3 1404 00833 1057

D0788777

WITHDRAWN
PROPERTY OF:
DAVID O. McKAY LIBRARY
BYU-IDAHO
REXBURG ID 83460-0405

JAN 1 8 2023

MAR 17 2002

Fishing

Paul Mason

Smart Apple Media

This edition first published in 2008 in the United States of America by Smart Apple Media.
All rights reserved. No part of this book may be reproduced in any form or by any means
without written permission from the publisher.

Smart Apple Media
2140 Howard Drive West
North Mankato, Minnesota 56003

First published in 2007 by
MACMILLAN EDUCATION AUSTRALIA PTY LTD
627 Chapel Street, South Yarra, Australia 3141

Visit our Web site at www.macmillan.com.au or go directly to www.macmillanlibrary.com.au

Associated companies and representatives throughout the world.

Copyright © Paul Mason 2007

Library of Congress Cataloging-in-Publication Data

Mason, Paul, 1967-
    Fishing / by Paul Mason.
    p. cm. — (Recreational sports)
    Includes index.
    ISBN 978-1-59920-131-3
    1. Fishing—Juvenile literature. I. Title.

    SH445.M23 2007
    799.1—dc22

                                                2007004596

Edited by Vanessa Lanaway
Text and cover design by Pier Vido
Page layout by Pier Vido
Photo research by Naomi Parker
Illustrations by Boris Silvestri
Map on pp. 28–9 by Pier Vido

Printed in U.S.

Acknowledgements
The author and the publisher are grateful to the following for permission to reproduce
copyright material:

Front cover photograph: Man fishing in a river, courtesy of Jordan Shaw/Istockphoto.

Photos courtesy of:
Stephen Frink/Corbis/Australian Picture Library, p. 20 (bottom); Stephen Booth, pp. 7 (bottom),
8, 24, 26; Anne Ackermann/Getty Images, p. 25; Magnus Fond/Getty Images, p. 30;
Johner/Getty Images, pp. 4, 21; Curtis Johnson/Getty Images, p. 7 (top); Mark Lewis/Getty
Images, pp. 22, 27; Ian Sanderson/Getty Images, p. 23 (top); Arthur Tilley/Getty Images, p. 18;
Melissa Carroll/Istockphoto, p. 6; Elaine Lanmon/Istockphoto, p. 13 (top); Courtnee Mulroy/
Istockphoto, p. 9; John Prudence/Istockphoto, p. 12; Piotr Przeszlo/Istockphoto, p. 13 (middle);
Jordan Shaw/Istockphoto, pp. 1, 23 (bottom); Jamie Wilson/Istockphoto, p. 14; Claire Francis/
MEA Photos, p. 10; Rachel Weill/Photolibrary, p. 20 (top); Photos.com, pp. 5, 13 (bottom).

While every care has been taken to trace and acknowledge copyright, the publisher tenders
their apologies for any accidental infringement where copyright has proved untraceable.
Where the attempt has been unsuccessful, the publisher welcomes information that would
redress the situation.

Please note
At the time of printing, the Internet addresses appearing in this book were correct. However,
because of the dynamic nature of the Internet, we cannot guarantee that all Web addresses
will remain correct.

Contents

Glossary words

When a word is printed in **bold**, you can look up
its meaning in the glossary on page 31.

Recreational sports

Recreational sports are the activities we do in our spare time. These are sports that people do for fun, not necessarily for competition.

You have probably tried some recreational sports already. Maybe you would like to know more about them, or find out about new ones? Try as many as you can—not just fishing. Also try biking, hiking, kayaking, climbing, and snorkeling. This will help you to find one you really love doing.

Benefits of sports

Recreational sports are fun to do, but they also have other benefits. People who take part in sports regularly are usually healthier. They find it easier to concentrate and do better in school or at work..

"The two best times to fish are when it's raining and when it ain't."
Patrick F. McManus, fishing writer

People often go fishing in beautiful places.

Fishing

Hooking your first fish is a great thrill. When the fishing line tightens, and then zips out through the water, it can be very exciting. Today, millions of people around the world are hooked on the thrill of fishing.

There are lots of places to try fishing. You might start at a local creek or **dam** and, eventually, go fishing in the great rivers and oceans. Wherever there is water, there will probably be an **angler** trying to catch a fish.

"If people concentrated on the really important things in life, there'd be a shortage of **fishing poles**."
Doug Larson, English athlete and writer, explains how important he thinks fishing is.

Fishing off a jetty with a friend is fun.

Where to fish

There are many great places to fish. If you live near the coast, you will probably start fishing in the sea. If you live inland, you will probably fish in creeks and dams.

Piers and wharves

Almost every town near the coast has a pier or wharf. Fish often gather near them looking for food or shelter. This makes them great places to fish. All you have to do is drop in a hook and line with some tasty bait and hope for a bite.

WATCH OUT!

People sometimes fish from rocks at the water's edge. This can be very dangerous, because of the risk of being swept away by waves.

Anglers often head for piers and wharves in the evenings or on weekends.

Fish looking for food in the surf will often bite your bait instead.

Surf beaches

Surf **casting** is fishing from the beach, casting a line out into the surf. Fish feed in the churning water near the shore. With a bit of luck, one will mistake your bait for its proper food. The equipment is similar to other fishing gear, but most people use longer rods for surf casting.

WATCH OUT!

Always wear a life jacket when fishing from a boat, in case you fall in.

Boats

Fishing in a boat means you can fish in areas you could not otherwise reach. A boat can take you out into the harbor, into an **estuary** or even to offshore islands. The boat can take you to almost anywhere you think the fish might be biting. Boat anglers use equipment similar to the kind used for fishing from a pier.

A boat helps you catch fish you would not find inland.

Tidelands

Tidelands along the banks of rivers near the sea are good places to fish. In hot countries these areas can have mangrove forests growing along the water's edge. Mangroves have tangled roots that are underwater at high tide. Smaller fish love to hide in the roots. Bigger fish come to eat the smaller fish, and anglers come to catch the bigger fish. Mangrove fishing is difficult and dangerous from the shore, but it is a lot of fun from a boat.

Rivers

Rivers are great places to fish. Study the river for a place where the fish might be feeding. Then cast your line and see if you can get a bite.

WATCH OUT!
Always get permission if you have to cross private property to get to your fishing spot.

Tidelands are home to many different kinds of fish.

Dams and lakes

One of the most popular places for fishing is on dams. Here you can fish from the shore, a pier, a wharf, or a boat. Dams often have fish put in them just for anglers to catch.

Small lakes can be great for fishing too. There are many different kinds of lake fishing, but the same rod you use for sea fishing will be fine on a lake, too.

"Even a fish wouldn't get into trouble if he kept his mouth shut."

Author unknown. Part of the trick of fishing is figuring out how to get the fish to open its mouth and bite your hook.

Dams often have plenty of fish in them.

Getting started

Hand lines are an easy, cheap way to start fishing.
A hand line is a fishing line that you feed out and pull in by hand.

Rigging a hand line

The line on a hand line is tied to the reel, then wound around it. The handle can be specially designed or just a thick stick. A simple way to rig your hand line is to tie a sinker at the end. Using another piece of line, tie the hook a bit further up.

When you lower the sinker into the water, it weighs the line straight down. The hook and bait hang higher up. Set the hook so that it dangles just a few inches above the sinker. This arrangement is good for fishing from a boat or pier.

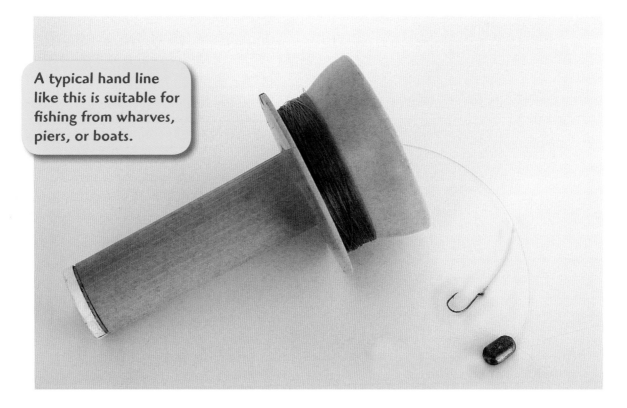

A typical hand line like this is suitable for fishing from wharves, piers, or boats.

Fishing from a boat, wharf, or pier

Hand lines can be used for casting out from a boat, wharf, or pier.
Hand line fishing takes some practice.

Technique

Casting a hand line

This technique has been used around the world for thousands of years.
You can use it for almost any kind of fishing. Always check there is
no one nearby who could get hooked on your line.

1 If you are right-handed, hold the handle in your left hand.

2 Hold the line in your right hand, about three to six feet (1–2 m) from the end.

3 Face the direction you want to cast. Twirl the line around like a lasso. Let it go.

4 Let the line run off the handle freely, then stop it when the bait hits the water.

Fishing gear

Fishing gear is called tackle. This is the equipment you use to catch fish and carry it home. Tackle includes a rod, reel, line, hooks, spinners, lures, sinkers, and a bucket.

Picking a rod and reel

There are many different rods and reels. To get started, tackle you can use for lots of different types of fishing is best. Ask local anglers questions to find out what tackle is best for your area.

- What kind of fish do people usually catch around here?
- What kind of tackle is best for catching them?

Many people start fishing with a rod and reel that can be used from piers, boats, and other areas where only a short cast is needed. A 6.5-foot (2 m) rod that can hold a fish weighing up to 18 pounds (8 kg), and a simple, fixed-spool reel should work fine.

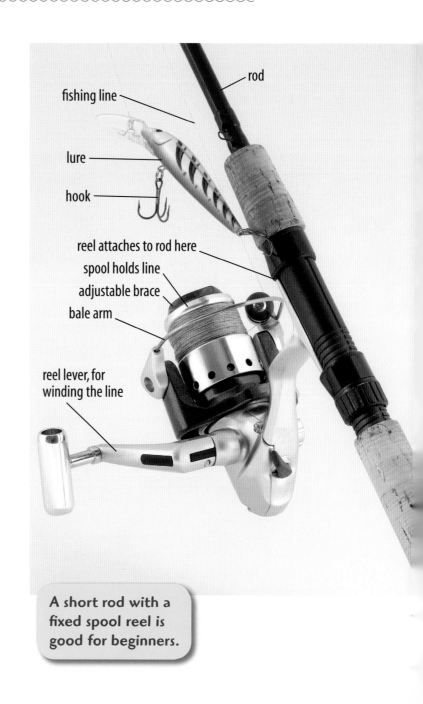

rod

fishing line

lure

hook

reel attaches to rod here
spool holds line
adjustable brace
bale arm

reel lever, for
winding the line

A short rod with a fixed spool reel is good for beginners.

Terminal tackle

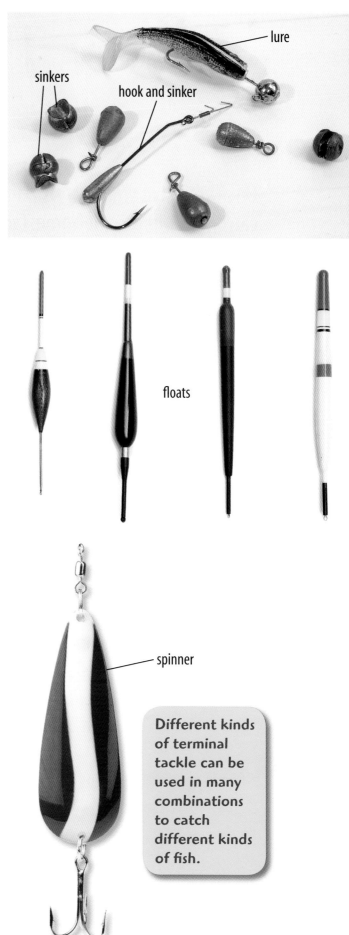

Terminal tackle is the equipment that goes on the end of your line. The tackle is attached to the trace, which is a finer piece of line attached to your line. If a large fish breaks your line, only the trace will break. You can set this up in the same way as for hand line fishing, but there are also lots of other ways. The three main setups are:

- with a hook at the end of the line, and a sinker further up to keep the line deep in the water. Sometimes there is a swivel between the sinker and the hook, to keep the line from tangling.
- with a **float** further up the line. The rest of the tackle dangles from the float.
- with a **spinner** or lure tied to the end of the line. These are designed to look like bait, so when you reel them in, fish are tempted to bite them. Only then do they discover your lure has a hook attached.

Different kinds of terminal tackle can be used in many combinations to catch different kinds of fish.

13

Setting up your gear

Once you have your first fishing tackle, you will need to set it up. Put your rod together, add line to the reel, and add the terminal tackle. You are ready to fish!

Putting your rod together

Most rods are simple to put together. They usually come in two pieces, and one piece pushes inside the other. The place where one piece fits together is called the joint. When the joints have been pushed together, you have a fishing rod.

The fishing line runs through little loops, called eyelets, on the rod. When you push the rod together, make sure all of the eyelets line up with the reel. That way, your fishing line will move easily.

A properly put-together rod has all the loops in line.

Top tip!

If the joints on your rod are loose, rub the inside part with candle wax.

Adding line to your reel

Many new reels come with line already attached. Even so, one day your line will snap or be damaged and need replacing. New line comes on a plastic spool. You need to wind it onto your reel.

Technique

Winding line onto a reel

Properly adding line to a reel will mean that the line will feed when you cast.

1 Pull back the bale arm on the reel. Tie the end of the line to the reel using a double slip knot.

2 Close the bale arm, and gently wind in the line. It helps if someone else holds the spool.

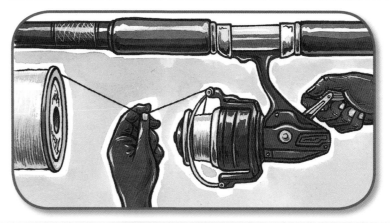

3 The line should be added evenly. Do not completely fill the reel. If you fill to the edges, the line can fall off and tangle.

Tying your hooks to the end of the line

There are lots of knots for tying a hook to the end of your fishing line. One of the best is the tucked half-blood knot.

Top tip!

Wet your knots before pulling on them. This helps the knot stay tight.

Technique

Tucked half-blood knot

1 Pass about 12 inches (30 cm) of line through the **eye** of the hook.

2 Loop the end of the line back over itself at least six times.

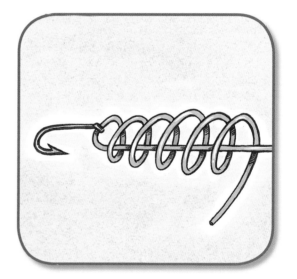

3 Bring the end of the line up through the first loop you made, then down through the big loop running from one end of the knot to the other.

4 Pull the knot lightly, wet it, then tighten it fully and trim excess line.

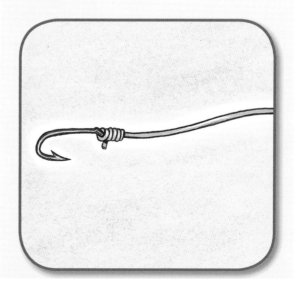

Adding a hook to the line

Sometimes hooks are tied farther up the line. You might have a sinker at the end of the line and need to add a hook farther up. A good knot for this is the stand-off loop knot.

Technique:

Stand-off loop knot

1 Make a loop four to six inches (10–15 cm) across.

2 Pass the end of the line through the loop.

3 Pass the end through five more times.

4 Tease the middle twist apart, and push the loop through it.

5 Holding the loop open, pull both ends of the line to tighten the knot.

6 Use the tucked half-blood knot to attach a line to the loop. Add a hook to the other end.

Sinkers and floats

Sinkers and floats do what you would expect. Sinkers are designed to make your fishing line sink. Floats are designed to keep the hook floating at a set depth. Both come in lots of different shapes and sizes. Some have a little hoop on the end for tying on your line. Others have a hole through the middle that the line goes through.

Casting

Casting is the technique of throwing your bait into the water. It is important to know how to cast accurately to get your bait to where the fish are feeding.

The long rods used for surf fishing can cast over 330 feet (100 m).

Basic casting

The simplest cast is the overhead cast. This cast can be used for all types of fishing, from piers, boats, and the shore. Before casting, check that there is nothing your line can get caught in, such as trees or power lines. If there are things in the way, cast from another spot.

Practicing casting

Practice your casting in non-fishing areas. When you do go fishing, you will be ready to cast wherever you want.

Top tip!

Although you can cast a hand line, a rod and reel helps you to cast much farther.

Technique

Overhead cast

1 Let out a little line from the reel. You want the end of the line to come about two-thirds of the way down the rod.

2 Open the bale arm on the reel. Hold the line against the rod. This will keep it from running out before you are ready to cast.

3 Check behind you to make sure no one is in the way. Take the rod back over your head and behind you. Tilt the rod slightly sideways, so the hook does not get caught in the rod.

4 Whip the rod forward. As the hook flies past the rod tip, lift your finger off the line. This will let the line go flying by.

5 As the hook hits the water, put your finger on the spool. When the line stops running off the reel flip the bale arm closed.

6 Wait a few moments, then reel in a few turns. This will tighten the line.

Finding fish

There are a few tricks to finding fish. If you can figure out where the fish are likely to be feeding, and what they are feeding on, it will help you catch them.

Choosing your bait

Choose bait that will seem tasty to the fish you are trying to catch. Bass eat worms from the seabed or pieces of crab. If you bait your hook with sea worms or crab, you have a good chance of catching bass.

This hook is being baited with live bait to attract the larger fish that eat them.

Piers and wharves

Piers and wharves are good places to find fish. These places provide fish with food and shelter. Prawns, crabs, and other small sea creatures live under piers and jetties. Larger fish feed on the small sea creatures. The larger fish are a good catch for an angler who has chosen the right bait.

Wharves are home to lots of fish.

Fish often feed in the waves at a surf beach.

Surf beaches

Waves coming into a surf beach disturb the small creatures that fish eat. Casting out beyond the third **breaker** often reaches an area where fish are feeding. You may also find fish feeding beside a rocky area. The surf disturbs creatures living on the rocks, and these are then eaten by fish.

Dams

Dams have lots of places where fish like to feed. The edges of the dam are often best. Try to find a spot where fish might hide or feed. These include:

- shady areas
- near bridge supports
- near dam walls

Top tip!

Fish are often easier to catch from a surf beach when the tide is coming in.

21

Hooking a fish

The most exciting moment in fishing is when you know you have hooked a fish. When this happens, there are a few tricks that will help you get the fish to shore.

Setting the hook

Setting the hook ensures that the fish is properly hooked. When you think you have a bite, give your rod a firm, upward movement. This will cause the hook to set, or sink into, the fish's mouth. Now the fish will not be able to swim off. Once the fish is on the hook, try to keep the line tight.

Using the rod

If a fish pulls strongly on the line, you can use the rod to help reel it in. Hold the rod up high, almost straight up in the air. The rod will bend toward the fish, taking some of the strain. Lower the rod and wind the reel, then lift the rod up again to pull the fish in. If you have caught a big one, this makes your line less likely to break.

This angler is using his rod to take the strain.

Fighting fish

Fish that try especially hard to escape when they are hooked are known as fighting fish, or game fish. Fighting fish are the hardest, and most fun, to land. They often take the bait very suddenly, unlike other fish, which nibble on the bait.

Some fish actually leap out of the water when they are hooked.

Technique

Hooking a fighting fish

Use these tips to help you hook a fish that fights against being caught.

1 When you set the hook, the line will begin to zip off your reel. The fish is running. Let it go. Keep your rod held high.
2 If the fish heads for a place where your line could get snagged, steer it away by pulling it sideways.
3 Once the fish slows down, gently begin to reel it toward you. Be ready for the fish to run again. If it does, let it go.
4 Repeat the process until the fish can be brought right in near you.

"The fishing was good. It was the catching that was bad."

A.K. Best, well-known angler.

Pulling a hooked fish sideways can save your line from being snagged.

Landing a fish

Once you have got a fish reeled in, you still have to get it to shore.
This is called landing a fish. It can be a tricky thing to manage.

Using a landing net

A landing net is a special net with a long handle.
Boat and shore anglers use them to land fish.

Technique

Using a landing net

Always have your landing
net within reach. That way,
you can easily grab it.

1 Bring the fish in as close
  as possible.
2 Slip the net into the water
  behind the fish, so you do
  not frighten it.
3 Lift your rod to guide the
  fish into the net.
4 Once the fish is in the net,
  lift it out of the water.

Bring your fish to
the landing net as
gently as possible.

Pier and wharf fishing

There is really only one way to land a fish if you are on a pier or wharf. Reel it gently up from the water. Then, swing the fish in and lie it on the deck.

When fishing from a pier, reel the fish up carefully.

Hook removal

Once the fish has been landed, you need to remove the hook. Never put your fingers in a fish's mouth. They have very powerful jaws. If the hook is deep inside its mouth, use a disgorger. These can be bought in any tackle shop.

"It is not a fish until it's on the bank."

Irish Proverb.

Releasing a fish

Some anglers let fish go after catching them. This is called catch and release.

Why release fish?

You may decide to release a fish for several reasons:

- The fish is too small to be kept.
- It might be a kind of fish that you are not allowed to catch.
- There may be limits on how many fish you are allowed to catch. These are called bag limits.
- It might be an **inedible** fish.
- You might decide that catching the fish is what you enjoy, but you may not want to eat it.

Top tip!

If possible, release fish into cool, deep water. This gives them a better chance of surviving.

Many fish have to be returned to the water if they are below a certain size.

Releasing a fish

If you plan to release a fish, try to land it as quickly as possible. This way, the fish will not get so tired that it cannot swim off later.

Technique
Releasing a fish

Follow these tips to release a fish without hurting it.
1 Use barbless hooks. These are hooks without notches on the end. These are easier to remove.
2 If you can, remove the hook and release the fish while it is still in the water.
3 If you do remove the fish from the water, use wet hands or a wet towel to hold it gently.
4 Try not to use a net.
5 Remove the hook as quickly as possible. If the hook is deep inside the fish, cut the line close to the fish's mouth. The juices in its stomach will eventually dissolve the hook.

If the fish does not swim away after a second or two, slide it gently back and forth in the water to help it recover.

Fishing around the world

Almost anywhere there is water there will be anglers.
These are just a few of the best fishing spots in the world.

Salmon and trout fishing
Name Scottish Highlands
Location United Kingdom
Description Probably the most famous salmon and trout fishing area in the world, with beautiful, but often rainy, scenery.

Fighting fish
Name Southern India
Location India
Description Southern India is home to the mahseer, a giant fish that can weigh more than 110 pounds (50 kg). Mahseer are famous for the way they fight against being landed.

Salmon fishing
Name   Pacific Northwest
Location   United States
and Canada
Description   The northwest
corner of North America is
famous for its salmon fishing.
When the fish swim up the
river to breed, anglers have to
watch out for bears standing
in the water looking for fish.

Reefs, rivers, or mangroves
Name   Queensland
Location   Australia
Description   Queensland
has almost everything an
angler could want. You can
fish from a boat in the reefs
and coastal mangroves or
head for the region's rivers.

Trout and salmon fishing
Name   Lago Nahuel Huapi
Location   Argentina
Description   The Patagonia
region is among the world's most
beautiful fishing areas. Trout and
salmon were introduced from
Europe a hundred years ago and
now live in many rivers and lakes.

Interview: Fishing crazy!

Dave has been fishing since he was nine years old. He now works in a fishing tackle shop, as well as guiding tourists to good fishing spots.

How did you get into fishing?
My mates and I got handlines that we used to dangle off the pier. We caught more crabs than fish, but we used to go down there most weekends. It just grew from there, really. As soon as we could afford to we bought ourselves rods and tackle, and started fishing in different places.

What is your favorite kind of fishing?
My friend Andy's dad had a boat. He'd take us out once in a while, and we'd go into the mangroves and spin for mangrove jacks. They fight so hard that I think they're my favorites.

Any advice for young anglers?
Well, I've spent a lot of money on tackle I didn't really need. Expensive tackle doesn't always help you catch more fish. It's better to learn about the eating habits of the fish in your area, and the tides. That way you'll put your bait in the right bit of water at the right time!

What are the best places to find out more about fishing?
Most libraries have good books on fishing. Local tackle shops usually have information about bag limits and other restrictions. The Internet is also a good place to find information about what's being caught in your area.

Glossary

angler

a person who goes fishing for fun, usually using a hook, line, and rod

breaker

a breaking wave

casting

throwing your line and bait onto the water in the direction you choose, usually using a rod

dam

Large wall that blocks the flow of a river; water from the river builds up behind the dam, making a lake.

estuary

area at the mouth of a river, where the water is a mixture of salty seawater and freshwater

eye

the small hole at the top of a sinker, hook, or float that a fishing line can be tied to

fishing pole

another word for a fishing rod

float

fishing equipment that keeps the hook dangling at a certain height

inedible

something that cannot be eaten, either because it is poisonous or tastes bad

spinner

spoon-shaped disc with a hook beside it that tricks fish into thinking it is a little, silvery fish

tidelands

areas where land is uncovered as the tide falls and covered by water as the tide rises again

Index